Book of Quotes

INTRODUCTION

It's normal to have difficult moments in life, but sometimes we create them in our minds. So change your attitude and open yourself to new possibilities

This book contains 70 inspirational and motivational quotes that will help you overcome a moment of weakness.

The quotes are not divided into chapters, e.g. those about motivation and those about positive thinking.

How to use this book? Just open it on any page and read the sentence there. That's all you need to know.

INSTRUCTION

The quote is spread over
two pages,

so you have to read both to
understand it.

The mountains are
only in your mind

Enjoy your journey!

~Progress Champion

The only wall you have to climb

is the one you create in your head.

Not every day is good,

but there is something good
in every day.

Life is not about what
happens to us

but how we react to it.

A candle loses nothing

by lighting another candle.

Think about how you will feel

when you succeed.

Don't try to save something that

is destroying you.

It always seems impossible

until it's done.

Dirty water doesn't stop
plants from growing,

so don't let negativity stop
your growth.

The magic you're looking for

is in the work you're avoiding.

Do it with love,

not for love.

Kindness is a language
the deaf can hear

and the blind can see.

Winning doesn't always mean
being first,

but it means doing better
than before.

Eyes are useless

when the mind is blind.

Be yourself;

everyone else is already taken.

Take a deep breath;

it's just a bad day, not a bad life.

All endings are also beginnings;

we just don't know it at the time.

Constantly thinking about what was,

you'll lose sight of what could be.

To change the world,

you must start with yourself.

You don't have to be great to start,

but you have to start to be great.

Do something for me,

rise again and give it your all.

Don't let the world's evil turn that
boy inside you

into someone you never wanted to
be.

It will hurt, hurt, and hurt

until one day it finally stops.

If you think you can, you're right.

If you think you can't,
you're also right.

Take a deep breath and remember,

just because you didn't receive
enough love in the past
doesn't mean
you don't deserve it.

Extinguishing someone else's candle

won't make yours shine brighter.

People don't understand

how much pain you had to
go through to be so calm.

Instead of thinking how hard
it will be,

think about how great your story
will be.

Your story may not start off happily,
but it's just the beginning.

The important part is
the continuation,
the one you write yourself.

The day you plant the seed

is not the day you eat the fruit.

If something costs you your mental
health,

the price is too high.

No one hears a tree growing,

but everyone hears a tree falling.

One day you will wake up

and there will be no more time to do
what you always wanted,
so do it NOW.

Rise and try again,

like the sun does every day.

You may fail,

but never give up.

Never wait for the perfect moment;

catch it and make it perfect.

Take a deep breath.

You forgave someone who didn't even apologize or regret what they did. That's strength.

Sometimes you don't know
the value of a moment

until it becomes a memory.

The most important day in your life
is not the day you were born,

but the day you find out why.

Be a good person without expecting anything in return;

do it for yourself.

The sun rises

even after the darkest night.

Don't climb the mountain
to be seen by the world;

climb so you can see the world.

Appreciate everything around you

before it turns into just memories.

I may not have a million friends,

but I have a few worth millions.

There's no secret ingredient
to make something special.

Just believe it's special.

Every day spent with you
is my favourite,

so today is my favourite day. <3

If you only do what you can,

you will never be more
than you are now.

You can start again,

like the sun does every morning.

Let your smile change the world,

but don't let the world change
your smile.

Elevate your words, not your voice.

It's the rain that makes flowers grow,
not thunder.

The past is a place to learn from,

not to live in.

How others treat you

is a reflection of who they are,
not who you are.

If you love something, let it go;

if it comes back to you, it's yours.
If not, it never was.

Use things, not people;

love people, not things.

Don't lose yourself

trying to hold on to someone else.

Our lives are shaped

by our thoughts.

For the world, you may be nobody,

but for someone, you may be
the whole world.

The person who moved the mountain

started by collecting small stones.

Don't feel guilty doing

what's best for you.

Stop creating problems

in your mind.

Everyone thinks of changing
the world,

but no one thinks of changing themselves.

You live only once, but

if you live well, once is enough.

One sees clearly only with the heart.

What is essential is
invisible to the eye.

Who you become is more important

than who you were.

Remember, you can't go back
and change the beginning,

but you can start where you are
and change the ending.

Rereading the same chapter

won't change the ending.

Speak to people in a way that
if you die tomorrow,

they'll be satisfied with the last thing
you said.

The beauty you see in everything is

a reflection of the beauty within you.

Do one thing for me

make the dreams of your
younger self come true.

Nothing is stronger than a person

trying to rebuild themselves

You can change the direction of your
life today,

but you can't change your life today.